HELP! I'M A SUNDAY SCHOOL TEACHER!

OTHER TITLES BY RAY JOHNSTON

Developing Student Leaders
Developing Spiritual Growth in
   Junior High Students
Free Gifts for Everybody with Gary Wilde
   (David C. Cook Publishing Co.)

HELP! I'M A SUNDAY SCHOOL TEACHER!

Fifty Ways to Make Sunday School Come Alive

Ray Johnston

Help! I'm a Sunday School Teacher!: Fifty Ways to Make Sunday School
Come Alive
Copyright © 1995 by Youth Specialties, Inc.

Youth Specialties Books are published by Youth Specialties, Inc.,
1224 Greenfield Drive, El Cajon, California 92021.

Library of Congress Cataloging-in-Publication Data

Johnston, Ray, 1952–
    Help! I'm a Sunday school teacher! : Fifty ways to make Sunday school
come alive / Ray Johnston.
        p. cm.
    ISBN 0-910125-16-3 (pbk.) : $7.95
    1. Sunday Schools. I.Title.
BV1521.J57 1994
268—dc20   94-44900
                                                                CIP

Edited by Noel Becchetti and Lorraine Triggs
Cover design by Church Art Works, Salem, OR
Cover illustration and interior cartoons by Krieg Barrie
Interior design by Rogers Design & Associates

Printed in the United States of America

96 97 98 99 00 /❖ DH/ 8 7 6 5 4 3 2 1

DEDICATION

With much appreciation this book is dedicated to three couples:

To Morgan and Sandy Davis

Whose contagious faith, support of our ministry and ability to enjoy life are changing the world from Moscow to Marin.

To Jim and Barbara Edens

Whose zest for living, generosity and faithfulness in service have given Carol and I great memories and wonderful support.

To Ron and Eunice Krieger

Whose commitment to Christ, excellence, parenting and each other has impacted not only their own family but ours as well.

TABLE OF CONTENTS

ACKNOWLEDGMENTS

A warm thank you to:

Tic Long—for staying focused on what really matters and consistently going the second mile.

Karl Grubaugh and Bill Romanelli—for their invaluable assistance in preparing the manuscript.

Kim Larson—for your keen editorial skills and love for our four kids.

Cindy Uhler, Stacey Wade, Norma Wilson and Pat Pankratz—for cheerfully handling phone calls, interruptions and overloaded work schedules with such dedication and grace that it is actually fun to walk into the office.

Noel Becchetti—for your willingness to go the second mile.

Bob Gaddini, Jeff Koons and Rob Dirkes—for your willingness to hang in there with kids.

Dave and Shelly Olson—for your partnership in the Gospel.

Burt and Irene Burgess—for raising the finest daughter and best wife anyone could hope for.

INTRODUCTION

IS SUNDAY SCHOOL WORTH IT?

It's 10:35 on Sunday morning. The service has just ended; the rest of the day's possibilities stretch out before you. You could head out to breakfast with friends, zip home to catch the big game, jam over to the club for a long-overdue set of tennis . . . .

Anywhere, perhaps, other than where you are on this fine Sunday morning—standing awkwardly in front of a small group of bored-looking kids who stare at the floor from their neat rows of chairs, chafing at having to wear uncomfortable clothes and at their parents, who ordered them to be there.

Welcome to Sunday school!

Sunday school classes like that (and we all have them) leave us wondering if God might be calling us to something easier—like being a sparring partner to Mike Tyson. They also leave us asking the one question that all teachers occasionally ask: Is this worth it?

Forty years ago, a Philadelphia congregation watched as three nine-year-old boys were baptized and joined the church. One of those boys was Tony

Campolo, now a Christian sociologist, professor, author, and world-renowned speaker. "Years later when I was doing research in the archives of our denomination," Campolo says, "I decided to look up the church report for the year of my baptism. There were three names: Tony Campolo, Dick White, and Bert Newman. Dick's now a missionary. Bert Newman is now a professor of theology at an African seminary.

"Then I read the church report for my year: 'It has not been a good year for our church. We have lost twenty-seven members. Three joined the church, *and they were only children*'."[1]

Only children! But add a few years of Christian nurture and, yes, a few years of Sunday school, and some of the children you're pouring your life into now may one day help shape lives around the world for Christ.

Sunday school *is* worth it. And I'm glad you think so too!

SECTION ONE

• —•— •— •— — •— •— •—•

FIFTY WAYS
TO MAKE
SUNDAY SCHOOL
COME ALIVE

• —•— •— •— — •— •— •—•

C.A.R.E.
GIVE YOUR KIDS CONTENT

● — ● — ● — ● — ● — ● — ● — ●

There are four elements essential to effective Sunday school classes: *Content, Action, Relationships,* and *Experience.* Together, they form the acronym C.A.R.E.

Traditionally, Sunday schools have been one-component events *(Content)* and have included little of the other three. This has led kids to believe that Sunday school is a boring, unfriendly place where they receive information but little else. Putting together a program that includes the four C.A.R.E. components will maximize your kids' learning (and they might actually like it!).

The process begins with *content.* What topics are you going to teach? Sometimes you will choose a topic because it's in the curriculum you are using. Other times it's because your kids need to hear it, or parents have asked you to teach it. Or you were at a convention and you heard Tony Campolo speak on it. Whatever the case, it's helpful to put some thought into the topics you plan to cover in a given time period.

Unless you are having a class that is strictly fun (and there's nothing wrong with doing that occasionally), providing good biblical content will enable your kids to discover what they believe and why they believe it. Whether you are planning an individual class, a four-week series, or your whole year, begin by asking, "What *content* do I want to communicate?" This question will help you to take aim on what you want students to know, feel, and do by the end of your class.

Once you have identified your topic(s), you are ready for the second step: Develop a plan of action to communicate your content.

C.A.R.E.
GIVE YOUR KIDS ACTION
• — • — • — • — • — • — • — •

When I think back on twenty years of Sunday school, one fact stands out: I can't remember *one* lecture. I do, however, remember the time we nearly froze when we met outside to learn compassion for the homeless, the time our class met in a local soup kitchen, debates on evolution and creation, learning the book of Jonah by acting it out, the sexuality question-and-answer session with an embarrassed newlywed couple, and having my faith stretched when I taught for the first time.

Many Sunday school classes are ineffective because we proceed directly from determining content to lecture. What could be a creative, diverse, action-filled learning experience becomes a boring monologue.

Think through your own faith development. What kinds of lessons do you remember? Which classes had the greatest impact? Most of us remember the lessons that required us to get involved, to do something.

Your Sunday school class can incorporate action simply by adding variety to the way you communicate. Object lessons, role plays, simulations, field trips, discussions, interviews, panel discussions, debates, workbooks, and learning games keep kids interested and increase the amount they will remember.

You will also be in good company. If Jesus taught his disciples the same way we teach Sunday school, he would have brought them inside, made them sit in rows, whipped out a flannelgraph, and lectured for an hour. Instead he opted for action. That's a model worth following.

C.A.R.E.
GIVE YOUR KIDS RELATIONSHIPS
• — • — • — • — • — • — • — • — •

A church growth specialist I know has a theory that he calls the *Friend Factor.* He maintains that people who visit a Sunday school class will make commitments to join if they *develop friendships* in that group. Those who visit and do not develop friendships will eventually leave, no matter how great the programming is.

Kids love being with other kids. In twenty years of running youth ministry programs, I have yet to have a student come up to me, retreat permission form in hand, and utter the words, "Ray, what will you be speaking on?" Their question (and determining factor in their attendance) is always, "Who else is going?" Kids want to go where their friends are and where they can develop friendships.

In some ways, Sunday school offers great opportunities for relationship building. You can start (or finish) each class with ten minutes of icebreakers. You have time to program a variety of fun team-building activities. You can form a welcome/follow-up team that writes thank-you notes to visitors and calls people who miss a class. Your class can celebrate birthdays and awards.

Helping your kids connect with each other will enable them to experience what Jesus meant when he said, "love each other as I have loved you" (John 15:12).

C.A.R.E.
GIVE YOUR KIDS EXPERIENCE

● ━ ● ━ ● ━ ● ━ ● ━ ● ━ ● ━ ●

A friend of mine told me how he recently let his young son fill the car with gas for the first time. He handed his son the pump handle and went inside to pay. He returned just in time to notice his son spraying gas all over the car rather than putting the gas in the tank. (Fortunately, no one was hurt!) As we laughed about his experience (and looked up car painting companies), I was struck by the obvious application to teaching Sunday school.

Spraying a car with gas may be effective if you are going to light it on fire, but it won't help the car go anywhere. The same thing is true in the realm of Sunday school. Our goal is to help kids get the truth on the inside.

You can begin by thinking through how your content can specifically help your kids. Ask questions like, "What do I want my students to *know, feel,* and *do*?" and "How can these kids experience these truths in their everyday lives?"

Secondly, give your students opportunities to apply what they are learning. Leave time in your lesson for application questions like: "How would your life be different if you applied this truth at home? At school? With your friends? In our youth group?"

The most important thing to remember about teaching the truth is that it's not what kids learn, but *how their lives will be different* because of what they learn.

P.S.: On page 124, you'll find an *Active Learning Planning Sheet* that can help you to plan an action-packed class based on the C.A.R.E. model. It's all yours—at no extra charge!

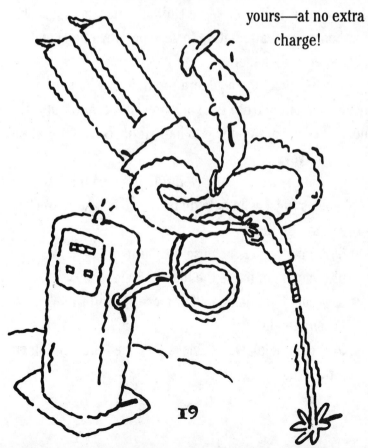

THEY MAY NOT BRING YOU APPLES
BUT YOU ARE NEEDED

Tony Campolo and Gordon Aeschliman have described how whole countries have moved through the process of being unevangelized, to experiencing and embracing the Good News, to abandoning the Christian faith.[1] This process, now going on in the United States, is especially hard on anyone attempting to develop convictions and character in teenagers.

You are teaching a generation that may be more in need of spiritual truth than any previous generation. The next time you are tempted to hang it up, consider that in a recent survey:

- 82% of the people surveyed said the idea that "God helps those who help themselves" is taken directly from the Bible
- 66% said there is no absolute truth
- 63% could not name the four Gospels
- 58% could not name half or more of the Ten Commandments
- 58% did not know that Jesus preached the Sermon on the Mount[2]

The lack of intelligent information about faith in our culture may lead kids to the conclusion that the Christian faith is simply not credible. Or more likely, they won't consider the Christian faith in the first place. When you sign on to teach, you inherit a group of kids at an age when they are *most open to Christ*. They may not bring you apples, but someday you will hear the words: "Well done."

ANSWER THE QUESTIONS YOUR KIDS ARE ASKING

Relevance and retention go hand-in-hand. Memorizing the books of the New Testament may not hold much interest to the third grader whose parents are divorcing. An in-depth study of the life of Hezekiah probably won't captivate the junior higher struggling to build friendships. Church history doesn't even wake up the high school junior who has just discovered his best friend keeps a gun in his locker.

Tackling the tough topics your kids are working through will help your kids understand the relevance of their faith. Don't be afraid to tackle the questions and issues they may be facing. For younger students these may be: What do I do when nobody likes me? How do I deal with a school bully? What do I do with my doubts about Christianity? How can I improve my looks? How do I handle my parents' divorce? How can I do better in school? Why can't I get along with my parents?

Teenagers may be struggling with questions like: Why no sex before marriage? How can God be just and allow innocent people to die? What about AIDS? What's wrong with drinking? Why shouldn't I cheat to get better grades in school? These are the questions kids are dying, sometimes literally, to have answered.

Warning: Make sure you check the really hot topics out with parents *before* you present them to your students. If you are doing a three-week series on sex, you may want to have a parents meeting (or send a letter) and give parents an outline of the material. This could save a life—yours!

If none of the above topics work, invite Rush and Hillary in for a debate.

KEEP YOUR KIDS GUESSING

• ━ • ━ • ━ • ━ • ━ • ━ • ━ •

It's Sunday morning in southeast Florida. It's hot. The room is stuffy. In a monotone voice, a Sunday school teacher reads Mark 2, the chapter about four friends who cut a hole in the roof to lower their paralyzed friend down to Jesus.

The comatose kids are bored stiff . . . until they hear footsteps on the roof, a chain saw start up, and the deafening noise of the chain saw cutting into the roof of their classroom. Roof tiles start falling. Kids scatter and dust flies, as four men cut a hole in the roof. They then lower one of their friends down in front of the teacher who smiles and says, "My son, your sins are forgiven. Rise and walk!" Just like that, this teacher has the most wide awake Sunday school class in the state!

(**Note:** The room in question was scheduled to be remodeled. Check with your pastor before trying this at your church.)

One of the reasons that kids are often underwhelmed by Sunday school is that it is just too predictable. They go to the same room, sit in the same chairs, use the same curriculum, hear the same stories, and look at the same

1948 map of the Holy Land on the wall.

When you break away from routine and make kids wonder, "What's going to happen in class today?" you'll have a class of alert, expectant students. The next time your students look bored, try the unexpected. Have people show up in costumes that represent the Bible characters you're teaching about. Have someone drive through on a motorcycle. Get prior permission and a change of clothes for your students from their parents, and at the start of class, announce that you all are going waterskiing.

Your kids will love the surprises—and, like the teacher in Florida, you will create some lasting memories.

WARNING: YOU MAY LIKE THESE KIDS

• — • — • — • — • — • — • — • — •

Chris was one of those kids in my junior high Sunday school class who stretched my teaching ability (and patience) merely by showing up. He had no interest in anything we were covering. His mouth was always open and his feet were usually in it. He was a constant distraction, and earned the nickname "Bugman" because of his habit of eating any insect handed to him by others in the class. He made me wish that he came equipped with a remote control, so I could hit the mute switch.

Several weeks after the class had started, his parents left town for a week (gee, I wonder why?) and for some unknown reason, asked me to take Chris for the weekend. I reluctantly agreed, and with visions of handcuffs dancing in my head, "Bugman" moved in for the weekend.

What a shock! We had a great weekend. Underneath the insecurity, I discovered a kid who was fun to be around. We played ball, ate junk food (no insects), watched movies, and had a blast. His love of conversation (which I hated in class) made him really fun to talk with.

About halfway through the weekend I was stunned to realize that I actually liked being with Chris.

I am long gone from that church, but every time I am back in town for a visit we get together. Keep an eye on the kids in your class. You might end up with some lifelong friendships.

WHEN IN DOUBT, SAY, "I DON'T KNOW"

As my four children grow up, they are asking some amazing questions: "How close do flies get to the ceiling before they flip over and land on their feet?" "How old is God?" "What's on the other side of heaven?"

The minute you sign up to teach (or parent), realize that you will be asked questions that you can't answer—like when my six-year-old son asked me why God would put a wet, dripping thing like your nose upside down over your mouth—there are some things we just don't have adequate answers for.

At times like those, don't be afraid to say, "I don't know." Being willing to admit that we don't have all the answers is intellectual humility and is a great gift to give your kids.

When you say, "I don't know," you create a safe place. It becomes okay to ask questions because you have freed students from the burden of pretending that they have to know everything. Students also will realize that not having all of the answers is part of life, and they can live for Christ *prior* to having every question answered.

They will also be forced to think for themselves. They

will exit your class with a faith that is their own. Maybe that's why Jesus often answered questions with questions.

By the way, I *do* have an answer for my kids' unanswerable questions—I tell them to go ask their Sunday school teachers!

TRY THE OUTRAGEOUS

• — • — • — • — • — • — • — • — •

As the offering was being collected at a church in my area, three men in dark clothing and ski masks burst in and announced, "This is a robbery. Don't anybody move!" After demanding the money from the petrified parishioners, they departed, taking the pastor's teenage daughter as a hostage.

After the thieves left, the pastor broke the news to his horrified congregation that he had staged the whole thing to illustrate how people who do not give ten percent of their income to the church are robbing God, as surely as the robbery they had just witnessed.

Perhaps the pastor at this church took this idea just a little too far (he's looking for a new job as you read this). However, there's little doubt he succeeded in getting the attention of his congregation.

Teaching the Bible to kids and keeping them awake at the same time is no easy task. One great way to do both is to try the outrageous. Recently I took several high schoolers from my class bungee jumping. Not only did we have their attention, but what a great object lesson on taking a leap of faith! (Note: Make sure you get parental

permission *before* you
embark on any outrageous
activities!)

HAVE FUN
IN CLASS

● ━ ● ━ ● ━ ● ━ ● ━ ● ━ ● ━ ● ━ ● ━ ●

A friend once visited a disaster of a youth group. The program was so boring, they came close to calling 911 during the bob-for-apples game because a couple of kids fell asleep and nearly drowned. Later, my friend learned that the church board had made it official policy that the high school Sunday school curriculum would be lessons out of the Heidelburg Catechism. (Like Dave Barry says: I am not making this up.)

Games and crowdbreakers—you use them to get your other programs up and running, so why not your Sunday school class? In fact, game playing may be even more useful in Sunday school, where a bigger percentage of your kids are probably there because someone made them come. Done right, a good game or crowdbreaker will pull down barriers and put smiles on otherwise less-than-sunny faces.

Many kids don't know how to have fun without doing something illegal, unhealthy, or electronic. One of the great gifts we can give kids is to create an environment in which they learn how to play together, laugh together, and have fun together. This type of atmosphere will attract kids to the Christian faith.

Ignore that little voice in the back of your head that keeps trying to insist that having fun on Sunday morning is somehow inappropriate. Go for it!

IT'S OKAY TO IMPROVE

● — ● — ● — ● — ● — ● — ● — ●

After teaching a Sunday school class, a seventh-grade girl (why are junior highers always so honest?) came up to me and said, "Ray, the lesson was fun—for about five minutes. Then it got really dull." After excommunicating her from the class (just kidding), I reflected on her comment and realized that I had put all the fun material in the introduction. I worked hard to *get* their attention but neglected to *keep* their attention. Her honest evaluation has helped my teaching so much that I am thinking about letting her return to the class.

The evaluation process enables us to discover how well we are reaching our teaching goals, and where we can improve our approach and methods. I occasionally tape myself in a class and listen to the tape later. Nothing makes me feel more uncomfortable, but I come away with a new sense of what I need to do to improve.

I also have my kids and colleagues periodically evaluate me. I give them the Teaching Evaluation Form on pages 118–119, have them fill it out after class, and then sit down with me and talk it over. Evaluation is seldom fun, but like medicine, its use can lead to growth and health.

LET YOUR KIDS CHOOSE THE CURRICULUM

Several years ago, I was frustrated by my kids' complete lack of interest in anything we did in Sunday school. While complaining to a friend who was a businessman, he cut to the root of the problem by asking one question: "Who decides what topics are taught in class?" He gently pointed out that people are the most apathetic when they have little or no involvement in the decision-making process.

The following week, I took the students out of the classroom and into my living room and took a survey. I gave each student a list of topics, and let them choose three that interested them most. I listed each student's top three choices, and then let the entire class vote on the totals. The six most-requested topics became our topics for the next six weeks in Sunday school. Miracles didn't occur, but I was shocked to discover a much higher level of interest in the following weeks.

Some kids are uninterested in Sunday school simply because they haven't had a say in what they are learning.

Taking a survey can help. You discover kids' felt needs and increase their sense of participation and ownership in Sunday school.

On pages 114–117, I have included my "Pick Your Topics" Survey, divided into four categories: *Bible, Spiritual Growth, Hot Topics*, and *Life Skills*. Use it with your class, or cook up your own survey. Either way, you'll see the interest level among your kids rise as they help choose the curriculum.

ADD LIFE SKILLS TO YOUR CURRICULUM

Bill loves Jesus. He has attended your church since he was knee-high to a communion cup. He has been on every retreat, says the right prayers, sings in the youth choir, looks forward to confirmation, has perfect Sunday school attendance, and is currently memorizing the Song of Solomon. But he doesn't get along with his friends, is flunking two classes, is always broke, and he can't balance a checkbook, change a tire, or use a computer.

As we develop convictions in kids, we also need to help them develop competence. For elementary school kids, this may mean learning how to keep their rooms clean or how to use a computer, how to play sports or how to handle money, or even how to get along with their siblings.

For teenagers, the possibilities are endless: how to manage a checkbook, how to tune up a car, how to change a flat tire, how to write a resume, how to apply for and get a summer job, how to manage time effectively, or how to get better grades.

You may discover that as students develop life skills, they will be able to use those skills in your Sunday school class. In my current church, some of the videos we show in class are filmed and edited by a high school student who learned how to operate the equipment at our church. (One of these days I may have him teach me how to set the clock on my VCR.)

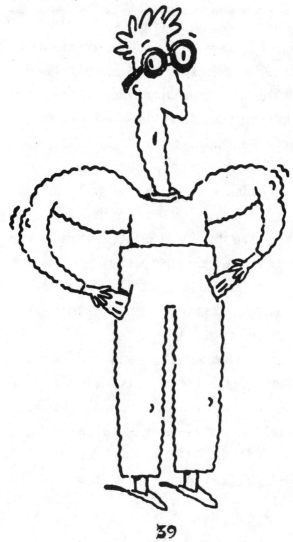

BREAK A MIRROR AND OPEN A WINDOW

Someone has described the kids we work with as the Kodak generation: overexposed and underdeveloped. These kids are also self-absorbed. Helping your kids break their mirrors can start right in your own Sunday school class. Younger kids can help with set up, room decoration, opening prayer and cleanup. Most older students can handle the welcome, lead games or discussions, and follow up with new visitors.

You can start a student leadership team that serves during your class. Create a few possible teams (welcome, follow-up, decorating, music, media, etc.) and let the students sign up. Take a little class time periodically to let the teams meet for planning.

Your class can also serve your community and the world. A junior high Sunday school class in the Midwest visits a nearby convalescent hospital every other week during class time. A childrens' class on the East Coast sponsors a child through Compassion International. A West Coast high school Sunday school class "adopts" a country each year. They put up a large map of that country in their room, give weekly weather reports of that country, pray for that country, and arrange for occasional in-class phone calls to missionaries in that country.

Opening the window of service can wake up apathetic kids and teach lessons that last a lifetime.

BRING IN EXPERTS

How would you like to give your students variety, introduce them to competent adults, raise the level of instruction in your class, and give yourself a break, all at the same time? It may be easier than you think. Just utilize the expertise that is in the pew right in front of you.

Every church I've been in has had people who were far more qualified to deal with some of the topics we were covering in Sunday school than I was. Many people won't commit to teaching your class for the next two years, but would gladly teach a one- or two-week series in their areas of expertise (rather than have their house TPd).

Here's how you can make the most of the experts in your church. First, bring in a wide variety of people. In my last church, we had a pharmacist speak on the effects of drugs, a cop talk about drinking and driving, a panel of parents talk about family issues, a counselor help kids deal with divorce, and a mechanic teach kids how to tune up a car.

Second, set up your expert to succeed. Put these people in their best light. Many are comfortable with their topic, but nervous about being with kids. Try some icebreaking activities such as interviewing them or moderating a question-and-answer time. Take care with your introductions and conclusions to help make the experience much more enjoyable and effective for all involved.

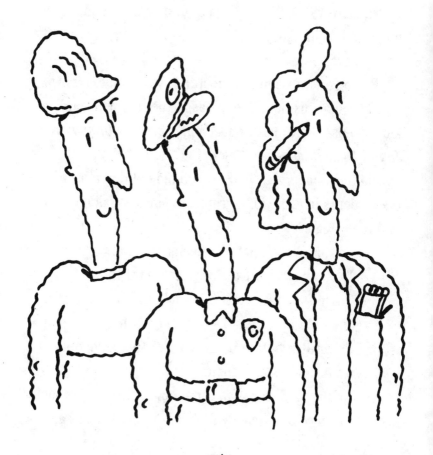

ALL KIDS
ARE NOT ALIKE
• — • — • — • — • — • — • — •

Sounds simple, I know, but my first few Sunday school classes were a disaster. I was assigned a class, handed the church-approved curriculum, and followed the instructions . . . until I realized that the curriculum and program had little or no relevance to anything my students were interested in.

Paying attention to the spiritual level of your class will enable you to customize your class to better meet your kids' needs. In my book *Developing Spiritual Growth in Junior High Students* (El Cajon, Calif.: Youth Specialties/Zondervan, 1993), I pointed out that most of the students in your youth group are going to fall into one of three categories:

> **Casual**—have not yet become followers of Jesus. Their level of spiritual interest may be low.
>
> **Curious**—have started a relationship with Christ and are interested in spiritual growth.
>
> **Committed**—are ready to serve (not students you would like to *have* committed).

One of the problems with contemporary Sunday school is our tendency to use curriculum written for curious and committed kids in a class packed with casual kids whose parents have made them come. A Sunday school teacher in California realized that he had more casual-level kids in Sunday school than the youth pastor had in his mid-week outreach meetings. He is now programming outreach events on Sunday morning and enjoying much better results.

CHANGE IS NOT A FOUR-LETTER WORD

A friend told me the following joke: "How many people does it take to change a light bulb in the church?" Answer: "Four. One to change the bulb and three to reminisce about how good the old bulb was."

Change is not a popular word in many churches. The motto seems to be, "As it was in the beginning, it now and ever shall be." And yet, keeping your Sunday school class a little off balance by throwing an occasional change-up can break monotony, raise interest, and produce growth.

Christian education specialist Marlene LeFever indicates that there is value in variety simply for its own sake by telling a story about a factory in the midwest with several creative managers. They did some experiments on ways to increase production. They added music and production went up. They added extra lighting and production went up. They took away music and production went up. They lowered the lighting and production went up. It became apparent that it wasn't the individual changes that were making the difference. It was change itself.

The list of possible changes is endless. Have kids face

a different direction. Meet in a different room. Change the class routine. Use different curriculum (or throw out your curriculum for a week). Move your class to the church bus. Swap teachers for a Sunday. Have your class put on a play for another class. Invite the parents in for a "Back to Sunday School" morning. Invite a Sunday school class from another church. Add music and food.

If your kids are getting tired of sitting in the same room, facing the same wall, and looking at the same 1948 map of the Holy Land, change may be just the prescription they need.

SMALL CAN BE BEAUTIFUL

● ▬ ● ▬ ● ▬ ● ▬ ● ▬ ● ▬ ● ▬ ●

You've agreed to teach a Sunday school class. You've prepared for several weeks, and now the big moment arrives. It's 9:45—time for class to start. The only problem—no one is there except you. You sit and wait. Finally, ten minutes later, a grand total of four kids are sitting uncomfortably on folding metal chairs, looking at you and waiting for class to begin.

Are you discouraged because your Sunday school class can fit into the back seat of your Honda? Don't be. There are some things you can do with a small Sunday school class that you could never get away with in a larger group.

You can actually get to know the kids on an individual basis. You can have discussions that include everyone, and you can share meaningfully. It's tough to remain anonymous in a small group because there's no place to hide.

Because you *can* fit your entire class into your car, you can decide to hold class at Denny's over breakfast. (Make sure to get their parents' permission beforehand.)

You can easily do other activities and projects together—volunteer at a soup kitchen, help in the church nursery, put on a short worship service at a nursing home, and more.

If your class is small, take heart: You have a ministry the same size as Jesus did. He spent the majority of his time with three people: Peter, James, and John. Who knows? One of those three kids may become your next pastor!

CONGRATULATIONS— YOU'RE AN EXAMPLE!

A little boy was asked by evangelist Billy Graham how to find the nearest post office. After receiving directions, Dr. Graham thanked him and said, "If you come to the crusade tonight, you can hear me telling everyone how to get to heaven."

"I don't think I'll be there," the boy replied. "You don't even know your way to the post office."

Like that young boy, your kids are probably short on affirmation and long on taking you for granted. But make no mistake about it—you are an example!

I know that you don't feel like a shining example most of the time. Your carpet doesn't have knee marks on it from a daily five-hour prayer routine. It's been months since you have worked on memorizing the book of Leviticus, and you haven't spoken at a citywide crusade in weeks.

Yet, it's the little things you do that make you an example. Being kind and gentle. Listening instead of interrupting. Remembering kids' birthdays. Providing a ride home. Your willingness to give those kids an hour of your week (which is exactly one hour more than most adults).

These look insignificant until you realize that they add up and are magnified because today's kids are starving for adults who care. Congratulations—you are an example! Someday, if you are lucky, they may return and let you know!

TAKE A BREAK

Most of us are busy. Too busy. Like Martha in the Gospels (a great Sunday school superintendent in her day), we get overwhelmed by our responsibilities, stressed by all we have to do, and guilt ridden by all we have left undone.

Sound familiar? The following one question self-test will let you know if you are too busy:

I prepared my last Sunday school lesson (check one):

___ During *Saturday Night Live*

___ In the car on the way to church

___ During the pastor's sermon

___ During the offering

___ In a donut shop instead of attending the service

___ During the opening announcements at the start of class

___ I didn't prepare, but got two really good ideas *after* class

If taking a short break from your Sunday school duties sounds like it will give the church authorities a heart attack, you can start small by arranging for a monthly substitute. Recruit a friend (or a former friend) to take the first Sunday of the month. Give the person all the tools he or she needs, and then go away for the weekend.

You may also want to take a summer vacation. Find returning college students or a group of teachers who have the summer free and practice the lost art of D & D (Delegate and Disappear). The break will do you and your sanity some good—and make you a better teacher when you return.

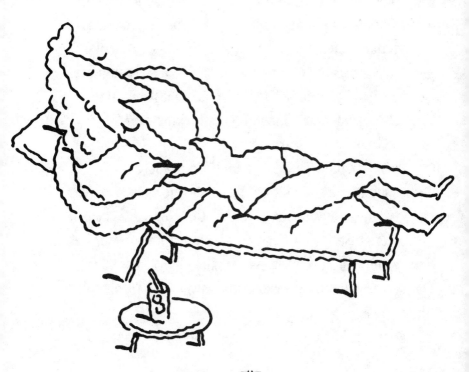

CREATE A PLACE TO BELONG

How many times have you been to a church youth event and the first thing communicated is the rules? The entire meeting begins on a negative note. We communicate to the kids, "Hey, this event is an adult event, you are lucky to be here, and we expect you to act in such a way as to make it easy for us."

Many kids feel as if they are stepping into a foreign environment when they walk into church. The music is unfamiliar. The language seems foreign. The sanctuary looks like a prison cell, and for most kids, a thirty-minute sermon could be titled "The Half-Hour that Went on for Days." You can help change this by making your Sunday school environment warm and inviting.

It's not that difficult to create a kid-friendly atmosphere. Have music or videos playing as kids arrive. Arrange the chairs in circles rather than rows. Replace that ever-present Holy Land map with pictures of your kids and posters for upcoming events. Set up board or table games throughout your room and have food waiting as they arrive.

Recently, I had the privilege to teach in a classroom

set up by a Sunday school teacher committed to giving his kids a sense of belonging. Stapled to the wall of the room were lunch bags with the name of each kid. The sign above the bags invited students to write each other encouraging notes and drop them into the bags. Every week he writes a note of encouragement to each one of his kids. The atmosphere was electric!

DISAGREEMENT CAN BE BEAUTIFUL

• — • — • — • — • — • — • — •

In many Sunday school classes disagreement is considered an act of rebellion. The result is a generation of kids who lack the ability to think for themselves and whose foundation for faith might be, "Jesus loves me, this I know, for my Sunday school teacher told me so." Unexamined and unquestioned faith often doesn't survive the questions raised in later years.

When you're willing to encourage disagreement, you'll enable kids to be honest about their doubts, process their questions, and develop a faith that they will own.

One way to do this is to set up in-class debates, which are wonderful for encouraging thinking. Several formats work well. You might try debating your class. You take one side of an issue, your class takes the other, and then go at it.

Or you can have the students debate each other. Bring in materials on a controversial subject (like evolution vs. creation), divide the class in half, and give each side a position to defend. Give the kids thirty minutes to prepare and thirty minutes to debate.

This teaching style is particularly effective with

adolescents. Kids who are too cool to listen in class are seldom hesitant to disagree. I have seen debates wake up an entire class of apathetic kids and observed actual thinking take place. For some kids that is a wonderful start!

EVERYONE BOMBS OCCASIONALLY

Okay, the Christmas story drama for your class didn't turn out quite how you'd hoped. Next time, you'll know to leave the goat out of it. For now, the kids are depressed, the parents want you committed, *you* want to be committed, and the aroma in your room isn't coming from the Christmas boughs.

Or (and maybe a little more likely) your class attendance has been dropping. The kids who do come seem bored, and when one kid asked why he should believe in God, you weren't sure what to say. To make it worse, that kid wasn't in class the following Sunday.

Failure is never fatal—but discouragement can be! When I bomb (and it happens regularly), I find that two reminders keep me going.

First, no teacher can connect with *every* kid. No Sunday school teacher is interesting every week. And no Sunday school teacher is liked by all the kids. You will have kids that are too cool, too flaky, or too bored—or they just won't like you. Give yourself a break. Chances are, if you are really honest, you don't like every kid either.

Second, no kid is beyond God's reach. Have you thought about the disciples lately? Doubting Thomas, loud-mouthed Peter, and James and John always arguing over who was the greatest. Sound familiar? The next time you are ready to throw in the towel, remember the disciples and trust God to use you to reach your students in his timing.

EXPECT GREAT THINGS FROM YOUR KIDS
● ━ ● ━ ● ━ ● ━ ● ━ ● ━ ● ━ ●

In a study a few years ago, a teacher was told she had several exceptionally bright and several exceptionally slow students in her class. In reality, the students were randomly selected. What happened? The "bright" students were called on more often, received more one-on-one attention, and got better grades than the rest of the class. The "slow" students weren't called on when they raised their hands, were chastised instead of encouraged, and received lower grades than their classmates. Eventually, *they quit trying and became the failures they were expected to be.*

I recently taught a series on discovering your spiritual gifts to a group of eleven teenagers. My students were sleeping through the material until I had each teenager sit at the head of the class and take notes while the whole group shared what they thought their gifts might be.

The whole atmosphere of the class changed! When they discovered that their friends actually believed that they possessed gifts and abilities, their confidence and interest level rose. Two of the students, Ben and Stacy, have actually started a lunchtime Bible study that attracts up to thirty classmates.

Not every kid in your class (or mine) will experience that type of transformation. However, teachers who believe in what their students can become raise the ceiling on their kids' possibilities for growth.

That lump of coal occupying one of the chairs in your Sunday school class may be a diamond in waiting.

GET YOUR CLASS INVOLVED

In *Keeping Your Teens in Touch With God* (Elgin Il.: David C. Cook, 1988), Robert Laurent researched the top ten reasons kids turn away from the church. To his surprise, he discovered the number one reason cited by kids was "lack of opportunity for meaningful church involvement." Most teenagers are convinced that there is little place for them in the church, and even less opportunity for service and leadership.

Positive faith is best taught in the context of commitment, service, and involvement. Those three essentials thrive when we create opportunities for students to make an impact.

The best way to make this shift is to get your class involved in service and leadership. The possibilities are endless. Younger kids can make posters, make and deliver presents to shut-ins, or help with many aspects of the class. Older students can provide leadership to almost any part of the class (welcome, announcements, food, teaching) or take part in whole-class projects such as sponsoring a child or visiting convalescent homes. The results are usually consistent—total chaos and spiritual growth. What a great combination!

GET YOUR KIDS TALKING

• — • — • — • — • — • — • — •

There you are, in front of the class, lecturing away on how Saul was persecuting the Christians, then to wake the kids up you ask, "Okay, now what happened to Saul?" Unfortunately, it is at that exact moment that every student has become utterly fascinated with his or her shoes, except the one kid whose eyes are so glazed over that you wonder if they're made out of plastic.

This situation plagues even the best teachers. Discussion-oriented classes are more fun, but require actual conversation. How did Sunday school become the only hour of the week that teenagers shut up?

One of the problems we run into is that by the time kids have been in Sunday school a few years, they learn the ropes. And one of the first rules of survival is to keep your mouth closed.

Breaking the "no-talk" rule may require a little creativity. Simply asking questions doesn't guarantee students will break out in actual conversation. Start kids off with their favorite subject—themselves. Go around the room and have them say their names, where they go to school, and their favorite movies.

Pair kids off for one-on-one discussions. That way they have to talk. After talking in twos, they are more likely to talk in the whole group. And when a discussion veers off the subject (and it will), resist the temptation to cut it off too quickly. When all else fails, give up and pick it up next week.

GIVE YOUR CLASS
A COOL NAME
• — • — • — • — • — • — • — •

A group of automobile analysts was recently given a car to test drive for a day. Led to believe that the car was built by Lexus, most analysts said they would consider buying the car. When told it was actually an Oldsmobile, they changed their minds. The conclusion was obvious. In the analysts' minds, Oldsmobile had become a name synonymous with outdated cars. Though the car looked attractive and performed well, buyers would stay away simply because of the name.

The same principle may be at work in your Sunday school. You have to wonder at the intelligence quotient of the marketing genius who thought a good strategy for teaching theological truth to kids involved making them get up early on Sunday morning, wear uncomfortable clothes, sit in rows, and listen to an adult lecture for an hour—and above all, calling it *school.*

Looking for a change of image? Test drive a new name. Ditch the name Sunday School and brainstorm other possible names (Prime Time, Sunday Morning Live, AM Stretch, Breakaway, etc.). Get additional ideas from your kids and let them vote. A cool name can bring new energy to your class, and your kids may find the ride exhilarating.

DON'T DECLARE—
DISCOVER!

● ▬ ● ▬ ● ▬ ● ▬ ● ▬ ● ▬ ● ▬ ●

Howard Hendricks, in *Teaching to Change Lives,* tells of a time when he asked a ranger in Yellowstone National Park about the frequent signs saying, "Do Not Feed The Bears." The ranger described how, in the fall and winter, park service personnel have to carry away the bodies of dead bears—bears who have lost their ability to fend for food.

Far too many Christians have grown up on a diet of sermons and lectures and have never learned to discover God's truth for themselves. They have memorized the "right" answers but lack the confidence or capability to learn on their own.

Shifting your teaching emphasis from declaration to discovery improves retention, creates interest, builds confidence, and contributes to long-lasting spiritual health.

Discovery-centered learning can be uncomfortable (it's tough to say no to a bear!). You will ask more questions and give less answers. You will discuss more and lecture less. You will encourage critical thinking instead of passive agreement. And there may be weeks where your kids just don't "get it" and leave the class confused. That's fine! It's part of the process of developing students who are capable of spiritual growth. Those students will be able to survive the sometimes long winter of doubt and arrive in spring with a faith that is alive!

GOD DIDN'T CREATE THE FLANNELGRAPH

•—•—•—•—•—͡—•—•—•—•

Guess what? Kids are different! I continue to
discover this obvious fact when I realize that my whole
class is never interested in the same topics or the
same teaching style. Students who love lectures can't
stand discussions. The kid who comes alive during
discussion falls asleep in lectures. The student who
loves games is intimidated by debates. The small
group that one student likes is lost on the student who
can't wait to get out on a field trip. What's a creative
teacher to do?

The incredible diversity of kids in our classes is
one of the most challenging aspects of teaching. It
also provides the greatest opportunity. By varying your
approach and teaching styles, you will reach more kids.

You can start by accepting the fact that there is no
"right" way to teach. God didn't invent the
flannelgraph (or lecture). That leaves us free to teach
in an amazing variety of styles. Speaking, debating,
serving, playing, storytelling, journaling, memorizing,

and questioning are just part of the wide variety of options. (For more options, see the Learning Styles Inventory chart on page 122.)

The next time you feel stuck in a rut, toss your church-approved curriculum for a week and try some new styles. (I promise I won't tell your pastor.)

HAVE AN ADVENTURE

Whether it's cable TV (105 channels) or ice cream (31 flavors), we live in a world where people enjoy a tremendous amount of variety. Unfortunately, that is the opposite of the average Sunday school experience. The typical class seems to be: gather, lecture, dismiss. Small wonder we are seeing little impact.

A good antidote for the apathy and a great way to shake up your kids is to have a class adventure. It might be as simple as taking your class of fourth graders to the police station and study the apostle Paul's imprisonment while you all are locked in a jail cell.

If you can find time, you may try something more elaborate and involved. In my last youth ministry, I took my entire Sunday school class to Mexico for a week-long mission experience. It took a lot of planning (I had no experience and didn't have a clue how to pull it off) and even more creative fund-raising, but most of our class went.

What an adventure! Our kids saw a different culture for the first time. They understood the effects of poverty in a new way. As they began serving, they discovered that

God could actually use them. They examined their values as they met gracious people who had few possessions, and who loved God and each other.

Some of our comatose church kids still haven't recovered from their week of service in Mexico.

HIT
THE ROAD,
JACK
•—•—•—•—•—•—•—•—•

I recently heard a cynical pastor describe the experience of Sunday school as "cramming little kids in a small room and teaching them to dislike God." While that may be a bit extreme, his point is worth considering. Most kids, if given the choice, would not opt for spending their Sunday mornings inside a classroom. A great solution is to hit the road.

Getting your kids outside the classroom and into a variety of learning settings is really an old idea. Jesus spent the majority of his teaching in non-classroom settings.

Move the class to your living room, a local restaurant, or the pastor's office. Some of the places you visit provide valuable opportunities for learning lessons. A trip to a cemetery is the perfect place for a study about eternal life. A meeting in a junkyard becomes a great setting in which to discuss materialism. A lesson on compassion might be best taught in a homeless shelter. Taking your class to a cafeteria is a wonderful setting to teach the feeding of the five thousand.

After all, it's tough to consider the lilies of the field if you can't see them.

LET THE INMATES
RUN THE ASYLUM

Here's a scary thought: Let your kids do some of the
teaching. Although it sounds a bit risky, there are several
benefits. First, getting kids involved helps combat apathy.
People who are active are rarely bored. When students
begin teaching, they become active participants rather
than passive spectators.

Second, students involved in teaching will learn more.
Involvement-based learning facilitates higher rates of
learning and retention.

Third, kids often listen to other kids much more than
they listen to adults. This means that the kids in your
class may also learn more.

Fourth, you may produce some future teachers. The
first time I was asked to teach as a high schooler, I nearly
had a heart attack. I nervously taught the class; no one
passed out, and I haven't stopped teaching yet.

Make sure to start small. Don't turn over the entire
morning and expect things to tick along like the gear
wheels in your Rolex. Let kids be responsible for pieces
of the puzzle—leading singing, setting up the room,
making the announcements, passing out songsheets,

setting up a skit, reading Scripture verses—and slowly increase their responsibility.

And remember, when things get chaotic (as they inevitably will), if nothing else, at least *now* they will know how *hard* it is to teach Sunday school!

IT'S OK TO HAVE FUN YOURSELF

●—●—●—●—●—●—●—●—●

Last year on Valentine's day, my wife Carol and I and four other couples boarded our church van for a group date. After traveling two miles, we husbands faked a breakdown on the freeway (very believable in *our* church van!). Just about the time our wives were starting to fondly remember their single days, a stretch limousine we had secretly rented pulled up behind us. We escorted our stunned wives into the limousine and proceeded to several stops where kids from our respective Sunday school classes served us different courses in our Valentine's progressive dinner. As we pulled away from each group, I could tell that the scene didn't quite compute in the kids' minds—actual adults having fun!

While my wife was surprised by the date, I was surprised by the response of my students. For these kids, seeing their teacher having a great time on a date in a limousine had a greater impact than any of my carefully prepared lectures. The next few weeks, as we joked about the experience in class, I could tell that some of their misconceptions about boring adults had been shaken.

Life is meant to be enjoyed, not endured. As Brennan

Manning says, "If you have the joy of the Lord in your heart, please notify your face!" A fun, joyful type of teacher will attract students to his or her faith and lifestyle. See you on the freeway!

KEEP A PRAYER NOTEBOOK

The first chapter of Mark records one of the busiest days in the life of Jesus—preaching, teaching, healing, the works. The next morning (I would have slept in), the disciples have to track him down because he has arisen early for prayer.

Prayer was one of Jesus' top priorities. When we pray, ministry becomes a cooperative effort. We are linked with God in the lives of people. I personally notice that when I am praying for kids, my expectations rise because I actually expect God to work in the lives of my kids. I worry less and enjoy kids more in those times when my prayer life is up to speed.

My own prayer life is more effective when I use a prayer notebook. Get a simple spiral notebook and put the name of one of your students on each page. Spend a few minutes in prayer each day for two or three of your kids, and record a note or two about how you prayed in the left-hand column. On the opposite side of the page, record how God is answering your prayers. You can even share with the kids how you see God working in their lives and mention how you are praying for them regularly. (It helps me to put a picture of each student on his or her page too.)

When I spend time in prayer, it reminds me that I am not teaching a class—I'm teaching Josh, Stacy, Ben, and Erica.

LEARN FROM YOUR KIDS

Growing up, I was so hooked on sports that I had little time to learn anything else. As a result, my carpentry skills are limited to knowing which end of the hammer to hold. So it was probably a mistake when my wife and I bought a home that was a candidate for fixer-upper of the year.

We moved in, bought all of the *Time-Life* books, began the remodeling effort, and took advantage of all the free help we could find. Most of that help came from our high-school Sunday school class. Several of the students had parents who were carpenters and knew more than I did about almost everything. They delighted in "teaching" their teacher the tricks of the trade and I loved the free help.

One of the joys of teaching is learning from your kids. Yes, they are experts at teaching patience, but students in your class can also help *you* in areas where they have aptitude. The list is endless—carpentry, computers, musical instruments, video games, or how to watch TV, listen to the stereo, and study at the same time.

My kids are also helping me learn spiritual truths. Kids teach me to deal with pain as I watch them struggle through the consequences of bad decisions. Kids teach me compassion as I learn to love kids that I am not normally drawn to. And kids remind me to believe in miracles as I watch Christ break through in their lives.

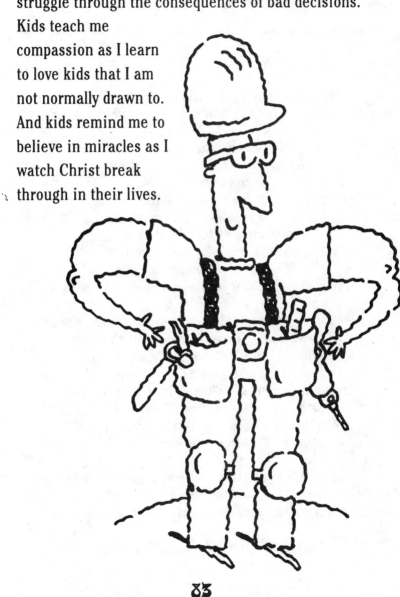

LET GOD FIGHT HIS OWN BATTLES

● — ● — ● — ● — ● — ● — ● — ● — ●

The Lesson

Then Jesus took his disciples up the mountain
and gathering them around him he taught them saying:

"Blessed are the poor in spirit,
for theirs is the kingdom of heaven,
Blessed are the meek,
Blessed are they that mourn,
Blessed are the merciful,
Blessed are they that thirst for justice,
Blessed are you when persecuted,
Blessed are you when you suffer,
Be glad and rejoice for your reward is great in heaven."

Then Simon Peter said, "Are we supposed to know this?"
And Andrew said, "Do we have to write this down?"
And James said, "Will we have a test on this?"
And Phillip said, "I don't have any paper."
And Bartholomew said, "Do we have to turn this in?"
And John said, "The other disciples didn't have to learn this."
And Matthew said, "May I go to the bathroom?"
And Judas said, "What does this have to do with real life?"

Then one of the Pharisees, who was present, asked to see
Jesus's lesson plan and inquired of Jesus, "Where are your
anticipatory set and your objectives in the cognitive domain?"

And Jesus wept.[1]

Yes, you have been given the awesome responsibility of teaching spiritual truth to kids. That's probably why you signed up! Some weeks are great—students are actually getting it; but most weeks your kids sound like the disciples in the preceding parable, and you leave class feeling like a failure.

That's the bad news. The good news is that it's not up to you to win every battle. Jesus is going to win some . . . and as a quick glance at the Gospels will confirm, he'll let some battles go. Your kids, like the disciples, will have tremendous ups and downs. The key is not to go with them.

The next time your kids leave you feeling like weeping, place them in the hands of God and let Him fight His own battles.

LIGHTS, (VIDEO) CAMERA, ACTION

I once attended a Christmas program at my son's school. The minute the play began there were so many video cameras pointed at the kids they probably thought they were at a Senate confirmation hearing.

Kids enjoy being in and making videos. What kid doesn't love seeing him or herself on TV? For creating interest, getting your students involved and developing future Steven Spielburgs, the videos your kids make may help them go from reel to real.

The possibilities for turning your kids into stars are endless. You can break your class into production teams, give each group a video camera and have them make a documentary on whatever subject you are currently teaching.

Or you can take your class to the local mall and let them interview people on camera. Your kids ask questions about topics you will be covering in class and tape the responses. Bring them back to class and view the videos. These kinds of videos make excellent introductions to your topic.

You can also use a video camera to help your kids gain familiarity with some of the events in the Bible. Bring a camera to class and have your kids create a video about a biblical event. Arrange an evening where the video is screened for your kids and their families. It'll be a surefire hit!

LISTENING IS A GREAT WAY TO COMMUNICATE

When leading seminars for Sunday school teachers, I occasionally will pair them up and assign roles, one to play the teacher, the other a student. I give the "students" one minute to invent and describe a personal crisis they are experiencing. I then instruct the "teachers" to demonstrate the worst listening skills they can come up with as the "students" share their worst crises. Afterward, I ask the "students" to describe how it felt not to be listened to. Words like *frustration, anger, insignificance,* and *hopelessness* usually surface. That role-play experience, unfortunately, can be a regular occurrence in many Sunday school classes.

Drawing your kids out may involve time beyond your Sunday school class. Set aside one lunch a month after your Sunday school class. Take a student out, bill the lunch to your pastor, and enjoy some one-on-one listening time.

Or, if you really want to shock your students, ask their opinions. I will never forget taking four junior high guys with me on a car-buying expedition (neither will the dealer). After taking the test drive, I pulled the guys aside and said, "Well, what do you think?" They had a blast giving their opinions about a car I actually bought—and they spent the next few years destroying.

In twenty years of working with kids, I have found that nothing says "I love you" as clearly as active, caring listening.

THE POWER
OF LOVE

• — • — • — • — • — • — • — • — •

At the 1990 National Youth Workers' Convention in
Los Angeles, a youth worker was moved by Tony Campolo's
story about throwing a birthday party for prostitutes in
Hawaii. He thought about a girl in his youth group who
was on the fringe. Her lifestyle was pretty wild, and she
felt isolated and alienated from the church. No one gave
her much attention. This youth worker asked if we could
call her during one of the general sessions. It was her
birthday and he wanted all 1,400 of us to sing "Happy
Birthday" to her.

We set up a speaker phone and he called her.
"Tricia?" he said in front of all the delegates.
"Yes," she said hesitatingly.
"Tricia, you are not going to believe this but I am in a
roomful of 1,400 people—
"You're kidding!" she interrupted.
"No I'm not. And Tricia, I was here at this convention and
I remembered that it was your birthday today and I asked
everyone here to help me wish you a happy birthday."
"You're kidding," she said, astonished.
"No, I'm not."

I wish you could have been there. Never have I seen a group of people sing louder or with more emotion, wildly cheering between each phrase. When it was over, there were very few dry eyes in the place. Tricia, for one moment in her life, knew that she was cared for.

Your Sunday school class is filled with Tricias who, by the attention you give, your desire to hang around them, and your affirmation, are discovering that they matter.

SURPRISE— YOU'RE ON THE CUTTING EDGE!

•—•—•—•—•—•—•

Author Charlie Shedd once said that when he set out to write a book on parenting, his titles kept changing.

• Before he had kids, the working title was: *How to Raise Your Kids*

• After his children were born, it changed to: *Ideas on How to Raise Kids*

• As the kids grew older, the title became: *Tips from a Fellow Struggler*

• And when his kids reached adolescence: *Anyone Got Any Ideas?*

Experience always provides perspective. No matter how great a teacher you are, your Sunday school class is not always going to be:

• a life-changing experience that rivals the best retreat your group has ever experienced

• your kids' substitute for seminary

• the largest youth gathering ever to hit your area

• your kids' favorite hour of the week, or

• *your* favorite hour of the week.

That said, Sunday school does offer a place where great ministry can happen. Sunday school may well be an idea whose time has come, because for most people, their first exposure to the church (and the Christian faith) will be on Sunday morning. If a family comes with kids, your Sunday school class may be their first exposure to Jesus. Your efforts may be the initial drawing card to motivate them to take a closer look at Jesus Christ.

OFFER
EXTRA
CREDIT

For some students in your class just showing up is a major achievement, yet you no doubt have at least a few students with a higher level of spiritual interest.

While you can't structure the class just for these students, it is helpful to remember that Jesus spent the majority of his time with these types of individuals. You probably don't have time to spend three years in the desert with these students, but you can offer "extra credit" for your motivated students that will help them deepen their relationships with Jesus and grow at a faster spiritual clip.

Start by developing a lending library. See if your church will give you a small budget (good luck), go to a Christian bookstore, and stock your own Sunday school lending library. Fill it with good books, tapes, videos, and CDs. Create a check-out system and let students have at it. Some of your students won't go near the thing, but some will take advantage of it. A good way to perk their interest is to take them shopping with you. This will also ensure that the library is stocked with items that interest them.

THERE IS STRENGTH IN NUMBERS

● ▬ ● ▬ ● ▬ ● ▬ ● ▬ ● ▬ ● ▬ ●

Sometimes, kids are going to get tired of you. (Hard to believe, but true.) And you are going to get tired of them. (Not so hard to believe.) Teaching your class doesn't have to be a solo flight. Whoever said you had to tackle this alone? Team teaching is easier, more fun, and gives your students a variety of role models. And you might be surprised to find that other adults (and students!) are willing to help.

Recruiting these fortunate team players can be a fun, affirming experience. In my last Sunday school class, I began by having the kids list on index cards all of the adults in our church that they liked and respected. I collected the cards and spent the next week showing these cards to those people whose names appeared frequently. Many of these people were now more than willing to help teach a group of kids. They enjoyed knowing they were liked, and I enjoyed the extra help.

Most people will not teach the class, but will help. Recruit others to handle song leading, icebreakers, follow-up, or teach one lesson a month. Or recruit teammates who will take over for an occasional Sunday or two or three. You get a break from developing curriculum, and your kids get a chance to see a new face.

TRANSPARENCY IS NOT AN OVERHEAD

•━•━•━•━•━•━•━•━•

After five years of marriage, a wonderful event occurred: my wife contracted pregnancy. We were thrilled. We phoned the folks and then had the privilege of announcing the good news to the kids in our Sunday school class. The next few days were filled with congratulations and kids lining up for lucrative baby-sitting jobs. Two weeks later, we began to sense problems with the pregnancy. The doctor confirmed our fears. My wife had suffered a miscarriage.

I hadn't counted on how tough it would be to share the news with our youth group. I went to the group determined to fake an example of the model Christian leader, praising God in tough times—but I just couldn't do it. I stood in front of the kids and all I could say was, "We're really disappointed, pray for us."

The students were amazing! They wrote us notes, baked us cakes, and told us they loved us. Our kids encouraged us through a tough time. They also began coming to me when they were hurting. Just being honest changed my relationship and ministry with those kids!

Kids aren't looking for perfect models. Kids are looking for real adults who love Christ and will love them.

CHALLENGE 'EM A LITTLE

I recently noticed a bumper sticker that said, "Hire a Teenager—While They Still Know Everything." Sound familiar? Let's face it, some of the kids in your class have been in your church longer than you have. Whether it's Leviticus or Luke the response is the same: "We've heard this before."

The best solution may lie in a phrase one of my seminary professors was fond of saying: "The task of teachers is to comfort the afflicted and afflict the comfortable." What your kids need to get out of their rut of apathetic familiarity is to be pushed, prodded, and challenged. Your content goals may remain the same, but by varying the action, you can wake up a class of longtime church kids.

For example, why not invite a homeless person into your class to talk about life on the streets? Or take your class to the local rescue mission and have them serve breakfast during class time.

I once took my junior high Sunday school class to a run-down day care center in San Francisco. They spent the day doing hard work (a miracle) and interacting with

Christians from backgrounds very different from their own. They learned lessons about compassion and service that they would have felt comfortable sleeping through in my usual class.

TURN ON
THE TUBE

•—•—•—•—•—•—•—•

When he was running for president of the United
States, Ross Perot used flip charts in every one of his
commercials to illustrate his point and make his topics
easy to understand. If there had been a way for Perot to
use his ears in a similar manner, he might have swept the
election.

We are working with a video generation. Movies,
videos, and television are primary vehicles for shaping
values in contemporary youth culture. The effect that
media has had on attention and retention rates is
extraordinary.

So why let the devil have all the good tools? Let's use
video to liven up our Sunday school classes. Tape a
segment of the news or a portion of a popular show and
have your kids discuss it as it relates to the Bible. Show
all or part of a secular movie. Movies like *Mississippi
Burning, Cry Freedom, The Mission,* and *It's a Wonderful
Life* have much to teach about issues of racism, freedom,
compassion, and hope.

Show good Christian videos. In the last few years, a
wide array of outstanding videos have come out which are

great for entertainment and teaching. I've listed some for you on pages 132–133.

Happy viewing!

JESUS CARES—
THROUGH YOU

●━●━●━●━●━●━●━●

Sunday school teaching encompasses a lot of tasks. We become attendance takers, counselors, lecturers, game leaders, discussion initiators, chauffeurs, activity directors, programmers, and more. In the midst of all we are doing, it is easy to miss our primary calling—to introduce kids to a relationship with a God who cares about them.

Brennan Manning tells a wonderful story about a young boy who was playing hide-and-seek with his friend. When it was the boy's turn to hide, he waited and waited for his friend to find him. Finally, he came out of his hiding place only to discover that his friend had gone home. He wasn't even looking. The little boy went home sobbing to his father, saying, "No one was looking for me."

The good news is that Jesus is looking for us and for our kids. Our primary task is to help kids hear and respond to that call.

I know what most of you are saying: "I can't do that. I'm not spiritual enough."

Recently, I received a letter from a college student. Six years ago, she became a Christian at a camp where I was speaking. Her letter was instructive. She wrote, "Ray, I want to thank you for being at our camp. The retreat changed my life. It meant so much to me when you asked me to send you my picture and said you would put it up in your office. *I can't remember one of your talks, but I will never forget feeling loved and appreciated.*"

When kids know that you care, the fact that God also cares makes a lot more sense. And God cares *through* you—just as you are.

YES—YOU CAN BE CREATIVE!

No one can be creative on demand. It's a lot like the person who comes up to me and says, "Say something funny." All of a sudden, the part of my brain that houses the humor library shuts down for remodeling.

Yet creativity is something that can be developed and strengthened, almost like a muscle. And it often takes a lot of bad ideas before you come up with a good one. A former student of mine who now works in advertising once said, "Creativity is ninety percent perspiration and ten percent inspiration." Every one of us has that ten percent. It's a matter of going into those dark corners of our brains to find it.

For those of you who struggle with your creativity quotient, start by giving yourself permission to go down in flames with a bad idea. No matter how badly an idea fails, no mistake is worse than giving up. If your first idea bombs, try another, then another, until one works.

You also may want to use the 3 Bs: *Borrow, Borrow, Borrow.* When you hear of a great idea, write it down and give it a try. I periodically meet with other teachers and we swap ideas about curriculum, games, icebreakers,

activities, etc. The end result is
usually more creative
ideas than I have time
to implement. A
wise, creative
plagiarist once said,
"The essence of creativity
is the ability to copy."

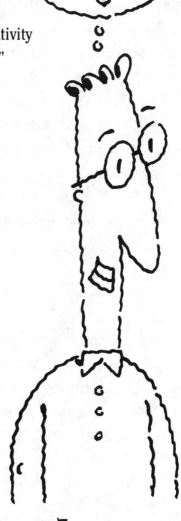

YOU, TOO, CAN BE COOL

Leith Anderson opens his outstanding book *Dying For Change* (Minneapolis: Bethany House, 1990) with the story of a declining church looking for a dynamic new pastor:

> A blue ribbon search committee did everything right to find the perfect leader. He was young but experienced, serious but witty, articulate but not intimidating, spiritual but worldly-wise. If anyone could turn this problem-ridden congregation around, he was the man.
>
> When the pastoral candidate first addressed the congregation, he gave an inspiring description of his qualifications, experience, vision, and plans. His final line summed up his stirring presentation: "With God's help, *I intend to lead this church forward into the nineteenth century!*"

Surprised and embarrassed by the candidate's apparent mistake, the chairman of the search committee whispered loudly, "You mean the twentieth century!"

To which the candidate replied, "We're going to take this one century at a time!"

Our culture changes rapidly, and our kids change with it. Keeping up-to-date is essential because yesterday's successful Sunday school program might be tomorrow's disaster. Keeping your Sunday school program from becoming a Jurassic Park exhibit begins by listening to your kids. Talk to your students outside of class. What are their needs? Their struggles? Their frustrations? Their triumphs? Then address their concerns in your Sunday school class.

Use up-to-date resources. Most food and medicines come with an expiration date. Sunday school resources should come with a warning: "Caution, this may lose potency if used after such-and-such date." Most curriculum companies (including the ones listed on pages 134–135) are happy to send you free samples. Gather these and let your kids select their favorites.

WHEN ALL ELSE FAILS, TRUST GOD

• — • — • — • — • — • — • — • — •

Whether you are teaching a restless roomful of squirmy elementary kids or a classroom filled with hormone-charged adolescents, visible results are usually hard to find. The Sunday school teacher waiting after class for kids to say, "Thank you for that message on Leviticus—it changed my life" may end up spending the night at church. If we are not careful, it's possible to conclude that God is not at work.

My first real exposure to the Christian faith occurred in a high school Sunday school class. The Sunday school teacher was a Christian cop (which I thought was an oxymoron). To my surprise, he was fun, friendly, engaging, and talked in simple language about how his commitment to Jesus Christ affected his life and relationships.

I walked away from that class still unsure about the validity of the Christian faith, but deeply moved and committed to check it out—*although in class, I acted like I was completely disinterested.* Twenty years later, I still haven't recovered from his clear, simple message.

It may seem that results are long on coming, but

remember you are not teaching alone. As you guide kids to Scripture, God is at work convincing students that his words are real and drawing these students to himself. Funny, I don't think I have ever told

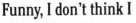

that teacher about his impact on my life. You may have kids like that. There are no apparent outward signs of life now, but twenty years later . . . who knows?

The People Who Brought You This Book...

┌───┐
— invite you to discover MORE valuable youth-ministry resources. —

Youth Specialties offers an assortment of books, publications, tapes, and events, all designed to encourage and train youth workers and their kids. Just return this card, and we'll send you FREE information on our products and services.
└───┘

Please send me the FREE Youth Specialties Catalog and information on upcoming Youth Specialties events.

Are you: ☐ An adult youth worker ☐ A youth

Name _____

Church/Org. _____

Address _____

City _____ State _____ Zip _____

Phone Number (_____) _____

The People Who Brought You This Book...

┌───┐
— invite you to discover MORE valuable youth-ministry resources. —

Youth Specialties offers an assortment of books, publications, tapes, and events, all designed to encourage and train youth workers and their kids. Just return this card, and we'll send you FREE information on our products and services.
└───┘

Please send me the FREE Youth Specialties Catalog and information on upcoming Youth Specialties events.

Are you: ☐ An adult youth worker ☐ A youth

Name _____

Church/Org. _____

Address _____

City _____ State _____ Zip _____

Phone Number (_____) _____

Call toll-free to order:
(800) 776-8008

BUSINESS REPLY MAIL
FIRST CLASS   PERMIT NO. 16   EL CAJON, CA

POSTAGE WILL BE PAID BY ADDRESSEE

YOUTH SPECIALTIES
1224 Greenfield Dr.
El Cajon, CA 92021-9989

Call toll-free to order:
(800) 776-8008

NO POSTAGE
NECESSARY
IF MAILED
IN THE
UNITED STATES

BUSINESS REPLY MAIL
FIRST CLASS   PERMIT NO. 16   EL CAJON, CA

POSTAGE WILL BE PAID BY ADDRESSEE

YOUTH SPECIALTIES
1224 Greenfield Dr.
El Cajon, CA 92021-9989

SECTION TWO

•—•—•—•—•—•—•—•—•

EXTRA CREDIT

•—•—•—•—•—•—•—•—•

"PICK YOUR TOPICS" SURVEY

The topics on the following survey are broken into four categories: *Bible, Spiritual Growth, Hot Topics,* and *Life Skills.* The topics at the beginning of each column are designed for younger kids, while those in the middle and end will work best with older students. As you develop your own survey, select from each section age-appropriate topics for your kids.

PICK YOUR TOPICS

INSTRUCTIONS: In each category, check your five favorite topics. Then star your top two in each category.

BIBLE	SPIRITUAL GROWTH
__Feeding of the 5,000	__God Made You Special
__The Love of Jesus	__Being Honest
__The Life of Jesus	__Learning How to Pray
__The Meaning of Easter	__How to Find Forgiveness
__The Prodigal Son	__Dealing with Doubt
__God Made the World	__Using Your Spiritual Gifts
__Is the Bible True?	__Does God Exist?
__The Book of Genesis	__Getting Along with Your Parents

BIBLE (cont.)	SPIRITUAL GROWTH (cont.)
__The Life of Moses	__Knowing God's Will
__Intro. to the New Testament	__What is the Church & How Do I Fit In?
__The Book of Acts	__Essentials of Serving God
__The Ten Commandments	__Prayer
__The Gospels	__Fellowship
__The Book of Nehemiah	__Making Your Personal Bible Study Sizzle
__Old Testament All-Stars	__Making and Keeping Deeper Friendships
__The Book of Jonah	__Understanding Spiritual Gifts
__The Book of Romans	__Getting Involved in Mission and Service
__The Holy Spirit	__World Service
__The Life of David	__Christian View of Marriage
__The Life of Joseph	__Missions Month—Getting to Know the World
__The Book of Ephesians	__Personal Evangelism
__The Book of Philippians	__Cults and World Religions
__Letters to the Corinthians	__Stewardship
__1 & 2 Thessalonians	__Taking On Temptation
__The Book of Proverbs	
__1 & 2 Timothy	
__The Sermon on the Mount	
__The Book of Psalms	
__The Book of Revelation	
__Know Why You Believe	

HOT TOPICS	LIFE SKILLS
__Dealing with the Class Bully	__Learning How to Make Friends
__When Mom and Dad Fight	__What to Do with Your Allowance
__When Kids Make Fun of Me	__How to Keep Your Room Clean
__When God Doesn't Seem Real	__Communication 101—Listening and Talking
__Homosexuality	__How to Handle Anger
__How to Survive Life at School	__How to Make Good Decisions
__Puberty—Look, I'm Changing!	__How to Study
__Stress	__How to Improve Your Grades
__Peer Pressure	__How to Manage Money
__Dealing with Your Parent's Divorce	__How to Practice Self-Control
__AIDS	__How to Use a Computer
__Drugs and Alcohol: The Choice Is Up to You	__How to Use a Checkbook
__Handling Failure	__How to Plan Your Future
__Depression	__How to Pick a College and Career
__Life in God's Family	__How to Say No to Partying
__Self Esteem	__How to Tune Up a Car
__Love, Sex, Dating, and Relating	__How to Change a Flat Tire
__Suicide	__How to Get in Shape
__Rock Music	__How to Write a Resume
__Loneliness	__How to Get a Summer Job
__Media	__Time Management: Balancing Sports, School, and Job
__Racism	

HOT TOPICS (cont.)

__Sexism

__World Hunger

__Vocation

__New Age Rage

__Handling Loss

__Handling Discouragement

__Evolution & Creation

__Abortion

__Euthanasia

TEACHING EVALUATION FORM

The following evaluation form is designed to help you critique your class in several areas: atmosphere, content, action, relationships, and experience. Have a couple of friends fill it out after observing your class, or have a couple of kids give you feedback using the form.

TEACHING EVALUATION FORM

Teacher's Name: _____

Topic: _____

Briefly comment on the following components of the class:

CLASS

    ATMOSPHERE: Was the class fun and enjoyable?

    CONTENT: Was the content relevant and interesting?

    ACTION: Did you participate?

    RELATIONSHIPS: Did you have opportunities to interact with others?

    EXPERIENCE: How will the content make a difference in your life?

TEACHER

Sincerity:

Enthusiasm:

MESSAGE (if there was one)

Volume:

Rate:

Eye Contact:

Did the introduction grab attention and motivate you to listen and apply the message?

OVERALL

What did you enjoy most about the class experience?

How could the teacher become more effective?

LEARNING STYLES INVENTORY

The Learning Style Inventory (Boston: McBer and Co., 1985) has had great impact on my teaching strategy. The inventory suggests that most students learn best in one or two of the following styles:

Experiential Learners ("Feeling")—intuitive and people-oriented. They learn best through relationships, creative expression, and personal experience.

Analytic Learners ("Watching and Listening")— reflective observers. They learn best by listening and watching.

Common Sense Learners ("Thinking")—logical thinkers. They are practical and learn best through strategies that provide time to process information: discussion, debates, questioning, meditation, and study.

Dynamic Learners ("Doing")—active experimenters.
They prefer learning experiences that allow for action:
participation, leadership, experience, games, and
serving.

In understanding these four styles, it is helpful to keep
two principles in mind. First, most people learn in more
than one style, but enjoy learning more in one primary
(their) style. Secondly, when we teach predominantly in
one style (like lecture), we are in danger of stunting the
growth of the students in our class who learn in other
styles. A great way to teach is to take your content and
ask the question, "How am I going to teach this in each of
the four styles?"

The following chart lists teaching strategies organized
by learning style. The next time you prepare for your
Sunday school class, try at least one strategy from each of
the four areas.

Experiential Learners ("Feeling")	Analytic Learners ("Watching and Listening")	Common Sense Learners ("Thinking")	Dynamic Learners ("Doing")
Game shows	Chalkboards	Agree/Disagree	Field trips
Discussions	Maps	Leader vs.	Research
Pantomimes	Interviews	Student debates	Dialogue
Illustrations	Overheads	Panel discussions	Dramatization
Music	Flannelgraphs	Case studies	Role-play
Personal sharing	Videos	Problem solving	Study
Simulation games	Stories	Questioning	Simulation games
Songwriting	Storytelling	Research	Making videos
Arts and crafts	Children's books	Inductive study	Teaching
Advertisements	Photography	Apologetics	Camps and retreats
Brochures	Laser shows	Guest speakers	Learning games
Murals	Acrostics	Paraphrase	
Posters	Memory work	Journaling	
Letter writing	Outlining		

A Learning Style Inventory Test is available from McBer and Company, 137 Newbury Street, Boston, Mass 02116, (617) 437-7080.

ACTIVE LEARNING PLANNING SHEET

The Active Learning Planning Sheet is designed to enable you to plan an action-packed hour incorporating the C.A.R.E. active-learning principles.

First, *brainstorm.* Set your Content goals, then brainstorm ideas for the Action, Relationship, and Experience components of your lesson.

Next, *plan.* Take your C.A.R.E. ideas and plug them into the six class components on the right side of the Planning Sheet. Add a little preparation and wrap-up, and you have an effective six-step process:

1. Preparation and setup (what materials and setup is needed for your lesson)
2. Opening (get kids connected)
3. Introduce the content (get their interest)
4. Explore the subject (get them involved)
5. Response (get it into their lives)
6. Wrap-up

ACTIVE LEARNING PLANNING SHEET

CLASS PLANNING & BRAINSTORMING (C.A.R.E.)	CLASS SCHEDULE
CONTENT Topic: Goal(s):	***PREPARATION & SETUP*** Materials needed:
ACTION What can we do to communicate the content?	***OPENING*** (Get kids connected) ***INTRODUCE THE CONTENT*** (Get their interest)
RELATIONSHIPS What can we do to build relationships during this class?	***EXPLORE THE SUBJECT*** (Get them involved) ***RESPONSE*** (Get it into their lives)
EXPERIENCE How will the kids experience these truths in everyday life?	***WRAP-UP***

SECTION THREE

●—●—●—●—●—●—●—●—●—●—●—●

RESOURCES

●—●—●—●—●—●—●—●—●—●—●—●

MY TOP TEN
TEACHING BOOKS

I have found the following books invaluable for philosophy and practicality. Your local library, church, or Christian bookstore can help you locate the following books.

Davis, Ken. *Secrets of Dynamic Communication.* Grand Rapids: Zondervan, 1991. Solid material on developing a theme, how to focus content, and how to communicate with your audience. The first half of the book is devoted to preparation, the second to delivery.

Hendricks, Howard G. *Teaching to Change Lives.* Portland, Ore.: Multnomah Press, 1987. Proven ways to make teaching come alive in the lives of students.

Hestenes, Roberta, Howard Hendricks, Earl Palmer. *Mastering Teaching.* Portland, Ore.: Multnomah Press, 1991. Includes great material on the task of the teacher, the challenge of Christian education, and the importance of evaluation.

Hestenes, Roberta. *Using the Bible in Groups.* Philadelphia: Westminster, 1983. A practical resource for anyone leading a Sunday school class or small group. This book includes Bible study methods that can be adapted to any size group.

Hybels, Bill, Stuart Briscoe, Haddon Robinson. *Mastering Contemporary Preaching.* Portland, Ore.: Multnomah Press, 1989. This four-part book covers today's audience, how to fill your messages with interest, how to deal with controversial subjects, and how to preach for total commitment.

LeFever, Marlene. *Creative Teaching Methods.* Elgin, Ill.: David C. Cook, 1985. My favorite book on creativity. Practical, with plenty of new ideas for communicating old truths effectively.

McNabb, Bill and Steven Mabry. *Teaching the Bible Creatively.* Grand Rapids: Zondervan, 1990. Covers thirteen key principles for teaching the Bible and gives dozens of ideas for how you can use each principle in your Sunday school class.

Murry, Dick. *Strengthening the Adult Sunday School Class.* Nashville: Abingdon, 1981. A good book regarding ten ways to strengthen adult classes in your church. Many of the principles are applicable to youth ministry.

Stott, John R.W. *Between Two Worlds.* Grand Rapids: Eerdmans, 1982. This gives an excellent history of preaching, contemporary objections to preaching and is the classic regarding balancing the tension of being contemporary and yet staying faithful to scripture. Contains a number of practical themes including:

preparation, study, and courage necessary to
communicate God's word to our generation.

Youthworker Journal, Summer 1990. This issue of the
quarterly is devoted to teaching. The articles are great
and the Youthworker Roundtable "Is Sunday School
Obsolete?" is especially helpful.

MY TOP TEN
TIME-SAVING BOOKS

These books have saved me time and increased the quality of my Sunday school classes. Most of these are worth twice what I have paid. I have listed these in the order of frequency of my personal use. Your local library, church, or Christian bookstore can help you locate them. (And yes, they add up to more than ten. So I lied.)

Bundschuh, Rick. *On-Site: 40 On-Location Youth Programs*. El Cajon, Calif.: Youth Specialties/Zondervan, 1989. Lesson plans for creative "field trips" to enhance classroom studies. Sample sites: garbage dump, cemetery, bakery, rooftop.

The Custom Curriculum Series. Elgin, Ill.: David C. Cook Publishing Co. Each book comes with five sessions, reproducible student handouts, clip art for publicity, and each is adaptable to your particular group.

LifeSources for Youth. Eugene, Oregon: Harvest House Fifteen workbooks on Christian life and Christian growth. Sample titles: *Putting God First; The Incredible Christ*.

Lynn, David. *TalkSheets*. El Cajon, Calif.: Youth Specialties/Zondervan, 1987–1995. This now seven-volume series, covering 4th grade through parents, each contain fifty reproducible creative discussions. Comes with a leaders guide for each TalkSheet.

Rice, Wayne. *Great Ideas for Small Youth Groups.* El Cajon, Calif.: Youth Specialties/Zondervan, 1986. Even in a larger church, Sunday school classes are usually small. I consistently turn to this book for ideas on how to make class fun.

_____. *Hot Illustrations for Youth Talks.* El Cajon, Calif.: Youth Specialties/Zondervan, 1994. One hundred great illustrations complete with application and supporting Scriptures. This one is a winner!

_____. *The Ideas Library.* El Cajon, Calif.: Youth Specialties, various. A wealth of information and the first resource I look to when teaching or leading meetings.

_____. *Up Close and Personal: How to Build Community in Your Youth Group.* El Cajon, Calif.: Youth Specialties/Zondervan, 1989. Includes a complete 13-week curriculum, 30 reproducible "TalkSheet" discussion starters, and 130 ideas for building community in a Sunday school class.

Tension Getters I and II. El Cajon, Calif.: Youth Specialties/Zondervan, 1981, 1985. Great material for beginning discussions, creating tension and getting students to think.

Yaconelli, Mike, and Scott Koenigsaecker. *Get 'Em Talking.* El Cajon, Calif.: Youth Specialties/Zondervan, 1989. Packed with ideas for breaking the ice and getting your kids to open up in class.

VIDEO RESOURCES

In the last few years, outstanding video resources have arrived and many are great for communicating the Christian faith. Your local Christian bookstore should have a growing supply of videos for the age group you are teaching. Several that I have found helpful are:

But is it Safe?. (Project Intercept, P.O. Box 720861, San Diego, CA 92172-0861). Filmed on location at Chula Vista High School, Miles McPherson does a great job of speaking about sexuality to churched and unchurched students at the same time.

Carmen Times 2 Club. (800/79-TIME-2). Video magazine format, topical, and comes with a leaders guide.

Edge TV. (NavPress/Youth Specialties, 800/616-EDGE). High quality, short topics, and comes with a leaders guide.

God Loves Me, So What!. (Family Films, 800/325-2004). Featuring Guy Doud, this creative video examines choices. Funny and fast-moving.

Next Time I Fall In Love Video Curriculum. (Youth Specialties, 800/776-8008). Featuring Chap Clark, this video deals with self-esteem, setting realistic sexual standards, breaking up, etc. Great as a four-week series or especially suitable for retreats.

The Question. (Mars Hill, 800/866-6479) A sensitive, powerful video about suicide. Comes with a discussion guide.

Selling Addiction. (Center For Media and Values, 310/202-1936). An outstanding, two-part video series that helps kids think critically about the alcohol and tobacco industries.

Sex, Lies & the Truth. (Focus on the Family, 800/932-9132). A hard-hitting video about the consequences of sexual choices.

Video Movies Worth Watching. Veerman, Dave (Baker Book House, 1992). This is a book, not a video, but it's a great resource for allowing your kids to watch and discuss popular movies. He covers seventy-five popular movies, evaluates each film's quality, and supplies discussion questions and Bible references for further study.

CURRICULUM PUBLISHERS

The best way to be creative is to use a variety of resources. Most of the Christian education publishers listed below are happy to send you sample curriculum and resources. Gather as many as possible and select those which fit your group and budget.

- CRC Publications (Christian Reformed) U.S.
  800-333-8300

- Cook Communications Ministries
  (Interdenominational) 800-323-7543

- Friends United Press (Quaker)
  800-537-8838

- Gospel Light Publications (Interdenominational)
  800-446-7735

- Gospel Publishing House (Assemblies of God)
  800-641-4310

- Group Publishing (Interdenominational)
  800-447-1070

- NavPress (Interdenominational)
  800-366-7788

- Our Sunday Visitor Publications (Catholic)
  800-348-2440

- Randall House Publications (Free Will Baptist)
  800-877-7030

- Regular Baptist Press (Regular Baptist)
  800-727-4440

- Rod & Staff Publishers, Inc. (Mennonite)
  (606) 522-4348

- Roper Press (Nondenominational)
  800-284-0158/(214) 630-4808

- Scripture Press (Nondenominational)
  800-323-9409

- Union Gospel Press (Nondenominational)
  800-638-9988

- United Church Press (Nondenominational)
  800-537-3394

- Wesley Press (Wesleyan)
  800-627-2537

- Wordaction Publication Co. (Nazarene)
  800-877-0700

- Word Aflame Publications (Pentecostal)
  (314) 837-7300

ENDNOTES

[1] LeFever, Marlene, "Only Children," *Covenant Companion* (September 1993): 13.

[1] Aeschliman, Gordon and Tony Campolo, *Fifty Ways You Can Reach the World* (Downers Grove, Ill.: InterVarsity Press, 1993): 126.

[2] Hendricks, Howard and William, *Living by the Book,* (Chicago: Moody Press, 1991).

[1] McNabb, Bill and Steve Mabry, *Teaching the Bible Creatively* (Zondervan/Youth Specialties, 1990): 19.

YOUTH SPECIALTIES TITLES

Professional Resources
The Church and the American
Teenager (previously released as
Growing Up in America)
Developing Spiritual Growth in
Junior High Students
Feeding Your Forgotten Soul
Help! I'm a Volunteer Youth
Worker!
High School Ministry
How to Recruit and Train Volunteer
Youth Workers (previously
released as Unsung Heroes)
Junior High Ministry (Revised
Edition)
The Ministry of Nurture
Organizing Your Youth Ministry
Peer Counseling in Youth Groups
Advanced Peer Counseling in Youth
Groups
The Youth Minister's Survival Guide
Youth Ministry Nuts and Bolts

Discussion Starter Resources
Amazing Tension Getters
Get 'Em Talking
High School TalkSheets
Junior High TalkSheets
High School TalkSheets: Psalms and
Proverbs
Junior High TalkSheets: Psalms and
Proverbs
More High School TalkSheets
More Junior High TalkSheets
Option Plays
Parent Ministry TalkSheets
Tension Getters
Tension Getters Two
To Do or Not to Do

Special Needs and Issues
Divorce Recovery for Teenagers

Ideas Library
Ideas Combo 1-4, 5-8, 9-12, 13-16, 17-20,
21-24, 25-28, 29-32, 33-36, 37-40, 41-
44, 45-48, 49-52, 53, 54
Ideas Index

Youth Ministry Programming
Adventure Games
Creative Bible Lessons
Creative Programming Ideas for Junior
High Ministry
Creative Socials and Special Events
Equipped to Serve
Facing Your Future
Good Clean Fun
Good Clean Fun, Volume 2
Great Fundraising Ideas for Youth Groups
Great Games for City Kids
Great Ideas for Small Youth Groups
Great Retreats for Small Youth Groups
Greatest Skits on Earth
Greatest Skits on Earth, Volume 2
Holiday Ideas for Youth Groups (Revised
Edition)
Hot Illustrations for Youth Talks
Hot Talks
Junior High Game Nights
More Junior High Game Nights
On-Site: 40 On-Location Youth Programs
Play It! Great Games for Groups
Play It Again! More Great Games for
Groups
Road Trip
Super Sketches for Youth Ministry
Teaching the Bible Creatively
Teaching the Truth About Sex
Up Close and Personal: How to Build
Community in Your Youth Group

4th-6th Grade Ministry

Attention Grabbers for 4th-6th
Graders
4th-6th Grade TalkSheets
Great Games for 4th-6th Graders
How to Survive Middle School
Incredible Stories
More Attention Grabbers for 4th-6th
Graders
More Great Games for 4th-6th
Graders
Quick and Easy Activities for 4th-6th
Graders
More Quick and Easy Activities for
4th-6th Graders
Teach 'Toons

Clip Art

ArtSource Volume 1—Fantastic
Activities
ArtSource Volume 2—Borders,
Symbols, Holidays, and
Attention Getters
ArtSource Volume 3—Sports
ArtSource Volume 4—Phrases and
Verses
ArtSource Volume 5—Amazing
Oddities and Appalling Images
ArtSource Volume 6—Spiritual
Topics
Youth Specialties Clip Art Book
Youth Specialties Clip Art Book,
Volume 2

Video

Edge TV
The Heart of Youth Ministry
God Views
Next Time I Fall in Love Video
Curriculum
Promo Spots for Junior High Game
Nights
Resource Seminar Video Series
Understanding Your Teenage Video
Curriculum
Witnesses

Student Books

Going the Distance
Good Advice
Grow for It Journal
Grow for It Journal Through the
Scriptures
How to Live with Your Parents Without
Losing Your Mind
I Don't Remember Dropping the Skunk,
But I Do Remember Trying to
Breathe
Next Time I Fall in Love
Next Time I Fall in Love Journal
101 Things to Do During a Dull Sermon